T0253087

HISTORY
FOR
PEACE
TRACTS

How do we understand what was, grapple with
what is and prepare for what is likely to be,
as a nation, as a people, as a community,
as individuals?

This series is an attempt to address this question
by putting into print thoughts, ideas and
concerns of some of South Asia's most
seminal thinkers.

In memory of Kozo Yamamura (1934–2017)

Is a Single Teachable Indian Past Possible Today?

JANAKI NAIR

LONDON NEW YORK CALCUTTA

The texts in this volume are updated editions of a lecture delivered at the 2018 History for Peace conference, The Idea of Culture, and a talk delivered at the workshop Between Teaching and Learning in December 2021.

Visit historyforpeace.pw to read similar resources.

Seagull Books, 2024

© Janaki Nair, 2024

First published in volume form
by Seagull Books, 2024

ISBN 978 1 80309 283 6

British Library Cataloguing-in-Publication Data

A catalogue record for this book
is available from the British Library

Typeset by Seagull Books, Calcutta, India

Printed and bound by WordsWorth India,
New Delhi, India

CONTENTS

Is a Single Teachable
Indian Past
Possible Today?

I am going to be a little irreverent to begin with.

It was in the 18th century that Indian History started. Indian History is a great number of wars in which the English fought victoriously against the Waratah Confederacy and various kinds of potentates called Sahibs, Wallahs, Jahs, Rajahs, Hurrahjahs,

Mahurrajahs, Jhams and Jhelhies. Most memorable amongst these were the terrible Napoo Sahib, the Maharatta of Pshaw, the Chandra Gaff and the Taj Mahal.[1]

This is a quote from a lampoon of history textbooks in Britain, published in 1930 but still a bestseller. In case you thought the authors were being imperialist and racist, here's what they say about the Industrial Revolution:

During the wars, many very remarkable discoveries and inventions were made. Most memorable among these was the discovery (made by all the rich men in England at once) that

women and children could work
for twenty-five hours a day in
factories without many of them
dying or becoming excessively
deformed. This was known as
the Industrial Revolution and
completely changed the faces of
the North of England.[2]

And if you'll indulge me another
excerpt, on Woodrow Wilson's peace to
end all wars, the 'Peace to End Peace':

Though there were several
battles in the War, none were so
terrible or costly as the Peace
which was signed afterwards in
the ever-memorable Chamber of
Horrors at Versailles, and which
was caused by the only

memorable American statesmen, President Wilson and Col. White House, who insisted on a lot of Points, including [. . .] that the world should be made safe for democracy, i.e. anyone except pillion-riders, pedestrians, foreigners, natives, capitalists, communists, Jews, riffs, RAFS, gun-men, policemen, peasants, pheasants, Chinese, etc.[3]

Why am I am starting with this?

When I was in school, one could read D. N. Kundra's history textbooks and with confidence state that Ashoka or Pulakeshin or Krishnadevaraya or

Serfoji II or a myriad of other jolly good kings planted trees, built roads and established chatrams, and one was assured of a few marks in the exam. I am certain I will never in my lifetime be able to essay such a lampoon of our 'Indian History', and not merely because of my own ability, or lack thereof, to satirize. We will never have our own version of *1066 and All That*, even though we have enough in our past to sustain more than a night's worth of stand-up comedy—imagine the fun we could have with Muhammad bin Tughlaq!

But I can also foresee the mob gathering outside my department should I dare to raise a laugh or two about the Tamil Nadu government deciding in June 2018 that state-sponsored school textbooks will stick to using Before Christ (BC) and Anno Domini (AD), rather than Before the Common Era (BCE) and Common Era (CE), lest they commit the historical sin of offending their minorities. In fact, this was a decision taken soon after their textbooks had been printed with BCE and CE used throughout.[4]

Our textbooks do not contain an agreed-upon account of the past. The historian Pierre Nora,[5] discussing the influence of the textbook *Le Tour de la France par deux enfants* (The Tour of France by two children) (1877) on the minds of millions of French boys and girls in the Third Republic, writes, 'Thanks to it, the Minister of Public Instruction could draw his pocket watch at 8.05 a.m. and declare, "All of our children are crossing the Alps." '— because one knew that they were studying history at school, that they were reading the same textbook, and that every child was taking the same tour of the Alps at 8.05 that morning.

A single language and a unified territory made this French textbook a sovereign text all the way up to the eve of the First World War. It is still in publication and still a bestseller. But in a place like India, a veritable Republic of Babel, has not every account of the past come forth from one or the other government in power?

The textbook has become an 'embattled object', or rather, more precisely, an 'endangered object'. The love of the past in India today is the stuff of battles in courtrooms, streets and movie theatres, rather than seminars, classrooms and journals. This passionate and personal engagement with historical knowledge is a particularly subcontinental affliction. The professional historian is herself something of an endangered species because the historical method seems to have no place in this 'love of the past'. I can thus end this essay right here, on the note that, perhaps, we should all only read and teach English history, Russian history or Chinese history, because it is no longer safe to try and attempt to teach Indian history—but I won't. Instead, I would like to proffer something on which I do not expect much agreement: a single, teachable past in India is no longer possible.

I will differ here from our former president Pranab Mukherjee who in his 2018 address to the Sangh Shiksha Varg of the RSS wove the myth of a single, teachable, usable past:

> Takshashila, Nalanda,
> Vikramashila, Valabhi,
> Somapura and Odantapuri
> comprised the ancient university

system that dominated the world for 1,800 years beginning the sixth century BCE.

[...]

Throughout this period of 2,500 years of changing political fortunes and conquests, the 5,000-year-old civilizational continuity remained unbroken.[6]

He did end on the note of our 'constitutional patriotism', but by that time the damage had already been done—for he waxed eloquent about the *sameness* of ancient India, before dismissing the entire medieval and early modern period:

Many dynasties ruled till the twelfth century, when Muslim invaders captured Delhi and successive dynasties ruled for the next 300 years. Babur defeated the last Lodhi King in 1526 at the First Battle of Panipat and firmly established Mughal rule which continued for 300 years.

I am basing my claim—that the Indian history textbook is no longer a possibility—on a number of challenges we are facing today, challenges from within the discipline of history, as more and more people feel the need to know their own past. Different regions, different histories, different castes, the South, the North-East, tribal people, Dalits, women are all asking questions: *Why not? Where were we? What if?*

A member of a community infamously designated as a 'criminal tribe' in the past wishes to study the origins of this appellation and how they came to be classified as a 'criminal tribe'. A student belonging to the snake-catching Iruliga tribe is writing a social history of his community in and around Ramanagara. A scholar from an agricultural background is researching the history of early modern agrarian relations in Chitradurga. Someone is studying the roots of underdevelopment in the Hyderabad–

Karnataka region, while another researches the history of the Bal Basappa performing cult and its message of equality. These are all examples of research conducted at a single university, the Kannada University at Hampi. And these are very local histories, local inquiries emerging from the questions students ask themselves, questions our history books fail to answer. Conventional histories do not explain to most people who they are or how they have got to where they are. A historian interested in answering such questions must develop or fashion new methodologies.

On the other hand, there are a vast number of communities that wish to exclusively claim individual historical figures as their own, with no regard for the results of the critical historical method. That is, nothing critical can be said about the lives of these claimed figures, and only a devoted member of the community can speak about them. Every outsider's account is perceived as a misrepresentation.

Examples abound from Karnataka alone: You cannot speak about Kanakadasa without being approved by the Kuruba Sangha. Sangolli Rayanna, for instance, can only be depicted by the Kurubas (whether Sangolli Rayanna is a Bedara Nayaka

or a Kuruba is still being debated).
Kittur Chennamma can only be
discussed by the Lingayats.
Kempegowda and even Kuvempu—
noted Kannada writer of the twentieth
century, winner of the Jnanpith
Award—are claimed by the Vokkaligas.
Koti and Chennaya, the Tuluva twin
heroes from the sixteenth century, are
claimed by the Billavas. I don't know if
this is a particular predicament in
Karnataka alone, but perhaps the
reader will recognize some
commonality in her region too. These
communities act as the gatekeepers of
knowledge about historical figures they
claim to 'own', their desire being to
monopolize all historical knowledge

about them. In light of this, it becomes virtually impossible to say anything about a number of such 'claimed' historical figures, particularly in the school textbooks. Should they be included in the syllabus? Should they be left out? Should only that be printed which has been approved and vetted by the community?

In 2006, I had contributed a chapter on clothing to an NCERT history textbook which briefly discussed the Channar Lahala in nineteenth-century Travancore, a struggle waged by Nadar women for the right to cover their breasts with clothing. During this period, both males and females considered to be lower down in the caste hierarchy were required to bare their breasts in the presence of higher-ranked members. This section from the textbook came in for a huge amount of political flak in 2012, six years after it was published.[7] The experience taught me what professional historians can no longer do. It taught me the limits of our capacity to intervene in questions that are so highly and deeply politicized.

More recently, Karnataka has been privy to further controversies about its history textbooks. In 2018, complaints were raised by some in the Hindu community alleging that the new revised ninth-grade history textbook was designed to surreptitiously convert people away from Hinduism since it begins with a chapter on the origins of Christianity and Islam (a very brief, basic and thumbnail sketch, I might add).[8] This chapter was followed by one which discusses various Hindu social reform movements in detail.

Another chapter on Tipu Sultan and Haider Ali exclusively focuses on the four Anglo-Mysore Wars (1767–1799) and how the two rulers reformed their army on modern European lines. There is not a single iota of reflection on the huge corpus of extremely sophisticated work done in the last 30 years on Tipu Sultan and Haider Ali by social and cultural historians, political and religious historians.

Yet another challenge to the discipline of history comes from above—the state and its obligations. Besides the central government and its preoccupations, especially in the last nine years, each state government propounds its own imperatives. In Karnataka, the last Congress government, for example, included a chapter in a school-level textbook on the value of folklore as a historical source. The inclusion of an entire chapter on this subject is not a bad idea at all, but it stuck out as a sore thumb in the book! There were no connections made with other discussions on sources in the textbook. This merely seemed to be the ambition of a particular textbook committee.

This form of interference in school syllabi is admittedly quite different from the examples we're familiar with, but I offer this instance to show how whimsical the addition of chapters and topics in history books has been, often driven by certain compulsions of the state.

Today, we can discern the characteristics of the Hindu-right from its pathological obsession with history, a preoccupation going back to the nineteenth century. Let us not by any means be deluded into thinking that this invocation of hurt sentiments (of which I gave an example a moment ago—the instance in Tamil Nadu) is something new—it has been in vogue at least since the beginning of the emergence of the textbook in India in the nineteenth century, with the British particularly warm towards entertaining various claims of hurt sentiments in the course of textbook production. It has more or less become the norm, as it were.

Technology is the other, newest claimant to the methods of history. The textbook is no longer the only source for understanding history. Rather, most people tend to consult 'WhatsApp University' for answers to their questions. There is a multitude of internet sources replete with dubious assertions, alarming claims and calls to battle on real and imagined historical heroes and heroines, on real and imagined wrongs and rights.

Moreover, there is a difference between the role played by the textbook and the classroom in the urban setting, or rather the urban middle-class setting, as opposed to the rural school where the textbook is the only resource. In the urban, elite context, for better or for worse, historical learning often takes place outside the classroom, to the extent that opinions about historical events and figures are ossified by the time students come across them in school. Judging by the feedback we received on the NCERT textbooks, students and teachers often overlooked those sections of the textbook that were intended to instil doubt or a sense of inquiry and criticality. Rather, they were fixated on the authoritative account of an event or a period, say 1857, that they believed to be true. As a consequence of this, these sections were frequently edited out, in order to preclude any ambiguity and confusion within the classroom.

In the rural setting, however, the textbook is perhaps the primary source of historical understanding about India. The first-generation researchers from Hampi I cited above are all coming to higher-education with the intention to produce new meaningful accounts of Indian history, fully aware of its potential influence in the classroom.

If the textbook is not doing the task of conveying a single agreed-upon account of the past, then what else can it do? We are living through what I think is perhaps the most dangerous time that is insisting on a single, usable, teachable past. And we are also perhaps best placed to intervene and say that there is a power to telling multiple stories.

I want to quote here the Nigerian writer Chimamanda Adichie who has warned about 'the danger of a single story':

Stories matter. Many stories matter. Stories have been used to dispossess and to malign, but stories can also be used to empower and to humanize. Stories can break the dignity of a people, but stories can also repair that broken dignity.[9]

We are perhaps losing our battle as professional historians because of our insistence on the protocols of evidence rather than focusing on compelling narratives. Stories are a vital necessity, especially in a country as diverse as India.

I am inviting you to share with me a reverie about method—

As teachers, our role as purveyors of information is probably over, what we must teach are the skills of thinking historically. The examples we use to demonstrate this are immaterial. I have argued elsewhere that perhaps we have spent too much time in the decades after Independence talking about the necessity of a scientific temper, and that it is necessary and important for us as historians to insist on the need for a historical temper. But what would the elements of such a temper be? Crucially, it must involve the ability to discern and compare contradictory sources.

I believe that is what the NCERT textbooks were attempting to do, and in that sense, they were revolutionary, allowing students a glimpse of how historians think, how they evaluate sources and so on. But this has to be implemented systematically and with patience—that is, qualitatively. Instead of approaching state boards to rewrite their textbooks, we should approach them to say that there should be no textbooks for the first four or five years of one's historical education. There should be no textbooks until you get to the board examinations. Rather, as an example, one could simply encourage students to say what they know by way of myths or epics and then ask them to compare that with a historical account, making them aware of this distinction. This calls for teacher re-education on a massive scale, which is an impossibility in a country of this size, given the variety of state boards, central boards, and now international boards.

This also calls for decentring the focus on examinations, at least in some subjects such as history, in order to empower teachers to introduce students to a historical method, rather than to state ordained historical truths. These are of course contingent on the existence of a consensual public sphere, which certainly does not exist in a richly diverse country such as ours.[10]

These would be desirable and revolutionary changes in the teaching of history, which also requires a demand from below, from parents, and teachers. At the present moment, such a pedagogical method is impossible, but that does not stop us from thinking of such alternatives.

The Future of Our Past:

The Textbook and Ways of Being Indian

I'll begin with what has changed in the way historians think and how history has become an argument about the past, rather than a mere recounting of historical facts. And I will do this by taking a few examples from the modern period, which is a period I am most familiar with. Then I'll briefly discuss the direction in which history writing generally and textbook rewriting in particular is now being driven. And finally, I will take some examples of state-level textbooks that have deployed innovative ways of thinking historically. So I'm moving in the direction of suggesting that we are facing insurmountable challenges in the teaching of history, both within the classroom and outside. And I am suggesting that our role as pedagogues should perhaps be to teach children and many others how to think historically, and what might that consist of.

In his seminal work titled *What Is History?* E. H. Carr wrote, 'The function of the historian is neither to love the past, nor to emancipate himself from the past, but to master and understand it as the key to the understanding of the present.'[11] To this, one can add, from the context of our subcontinent, that the function of a historian is not to seek retribution. Since our textbooks and teaching of history in schools and colleges has become something of a battleground, we shall begin by tracing the necessity of nation states needing this glorious, continuous past, and the textbook as somehow fulfilling this need. This need is not particular to India. This is true of all nation states worldwide.

Philosopher, former statesman and president of India Sarvepalli Radhakrishnan in the first report on higher education in 1948 had reminded us that 'we must give up the fatal obsession with the perfection of the past, that greatness is not to be attained in the present. That everything is already worked out and that all that remains for the future ages of the world is pedantic imitation of the past. Give up idolatry of the past, and strive to realize new dreams.'[12]

There has been a very creative period in the history of Indian textbook writing since the 1970s, when there were single-author textbooks by Bipin Chandra, Romila Thapar, Satish Chandra, Arjun Dev and others. But following the new National Curriculum Framework in 2005, textbook writing took a new turn. Since the 1970s, the practice of history has made great strides, because the functioning of our democracy has made people more conscious of their own pasts which may have been fractious and contentious. So we now have historical writing which is emerging from groups that have hitherto not had a presence in our understanding of Indian history.

We now know, for instance, that a lot was happening beneath the surface of the freedom movement in the name of Gandhi and non-violence, ranging from hostility towards his message (from the Hindu Right and the Muslim League), indifference to it (among Dalits in certain parts of India) and passionate embrace of his ideas, although in ways he did not intend (as evident from the Chauri Chaura incident). Gyanendra Pandey has shown how in 1942 Gandhi's slogan of *Karo ya maro*! (do or die) was converted to *Karo ya māro*! (do or kill), and it is important to reflect on this gap between the leader and led.[13] Fortunately, today we have access to alternative narratives and a wide range of new histories that tell us more about the freedom movement.

Secondly, we must also be conscious of the fact that our perception of the past changes over time. There cannot be a better example of this than that of the Bhima Koregaon battle, which is in the news for all the wrong reasons today.[14] This battle was fought between the Maratha Confederacy and the East

India Company on 1 January 1818 as a part of the Third Anglo-Maratha War. The small East India Company regiment, consisting of Mahars, Muslims, Marathas, Jews, Rajputs and others, was able to turn away the much larger Peshwa army. Although there was an obelisk which commemorated the bravery of those who participated on the side of the East India Company, this event that was more or less forgotten until 1927, when it was adopted by the Mahars as a symbol of a battle that they had won against the Peshwas. This incident comes to historical prominence when B. R. Ambedkar visits the site of the battle in 1927. Since then, there has been a

commemoration by Dalits at the spot.
It has definitely become part of the
historical memory of the nation for
some groups of people in West India.
And now there is some historical
controversy about whether any side
actually won the battle. Hence, we see
how democracy allows the voice of
people who had no history to assert
themselves in this national narrative.

Today we are also witness to a certain
straight-jacketing of history in which
the past is once more owned by the
state, which wishes to arrange an
antiquity for India that extends beyond
all known historical sources and
material artefacts. The attempt is to

erase the medieval period and reinterpret history as being only about *acche acche chize* (a past to be proud of) as one school teacher in Delhi put it.

The new challenges to our past come from the authoritative insistence that there can be only a singular understanding of Indian history—one that is authorized by the state and is upheld by the informal commentariat consisting of the hyperactive social media platforms that produce a consensus on the need for a glorious, ancient past. This could take the form of wiping out popular forms of commemoration, for example, by changing the names of places and roads, to excising some historical figures and events and inserting others, all in the interest of what have been called 'weightages'. It could take the form of narrowing the remit of history to political events and cultural inheritances, rather than to socio-economic structures, or even the ever-changing, conflictual hierarchies that are the staple of our subcontinent. Two controversies from the present will better illustrate this point.

In the 75th year of Indian Independence, the decision was made to delete from the *Dictionary of Martyrs of India's Freedom Struggle (1857–1947)* (which was implemented and completed by the Indian Council of

Historical Research [ICHR]) the names of 387 participants in the 1921 Moplah Rebellion. The former chairperson of the ICHR, Arvind P. Jamkhedkar, had explained the Dictionary Project thus:

> Our objective in the project has always been to try as best as we can to search for the cases from all segments of Indian society, and to bring into focus not only the known, but also the barely known, the obscure and the forgotten (especially from the lower rungs of society), and enlist martyrs into liberated India's roll of honour.[15]

You will agree that this is a very noble exercise and an example of social history at its best, where an effort has been made to go beyond the leaders and people whose names are more well known, to categories of people who may have been ordinary peasants, workers, homemakers and so on. This shows how the discipline of history has become much more nuanced and reflective. It was even acknowledged by another ICHR chairperson Professor Sabyasachi Bhattacharya, who commissioned these volumes: 'The question of inclusion or exclusion of some individuals may itself be a subject of controversy. Our decision was to make this compilation as inclusive as possible.' Moreover, and this is a very important point, 'The primary sources we have depended upon may contain errors of facts or interpretation, because,' and this what he points out, '[t]he inherent bias in the British-Indian government's records is too obvious a thing to elaborate upon [. . .]'.[16]

In other words, an effort has been made to overcome such data limitations. Yet, the names of the participants in the Moplah Rebellion were removed. This is because the event has been adjudged afresh, through the narrow prism of Hindu victimhood, and declared as a mere communal riot. While the uprising was one of the most serious threats to the British empire in

India during the Khilafat movement, it was also directed against the oppressive Hindu landlords, and there were sectarian elements in it. All serious scholarship of the Moplah Rebellion accepts that it represents a very dense cross-hatching of anticolonial sentiment, resentment against Hindu landlords who abused their economic and social power, a long history of lower caste conversions owing to casteist abuse by Savarna landlords and by their retainers such as the Nambudiris and the Nairs. There was rampant abuse of economic power wielded by these groups, like evictions, over-leases and increased taxation. And there were forms of religious humiliation by landlords which included destroying mosques and burial grounds and desecrating the Quran.

In other words, the reasons for this explosion has its roots in many different kinds of registers: the political, the economic, and, of course, the socio-cultural and the religious. Hence, it is not really possible to term it either as a political or a communal struggle. It is the scholarship of historians that has enabled us to acknowledge the intertwined nature of the event.

The second and very important recent instance of state ownership of the past has been in the context of the declaration of 14 August as Partition Horrors Remembrance Day. Let us remember what we learnt from the work of feminist scholars, which has been extremely insightful, particularly of Partition horrors. Feminist scholars such as Urvashi Butalia and Ritu Menon—I am just naming two—have shown that the displacement of millions, which was unprecedented in human history, the bloodletting and the misery was followed by a time when at least some women, on both sides, made their lives anew. But only to be freshly uprooted by the recovery of the abducted women undertaken by the two independent nation states—India and Pakistan. This was an operation of states on both sides of the border to rescue 'their' women. This imposition of an official kinship by the state on families and communities that had made many kinds of accommodations laid bare the state's claims on women's bodies as bearers, and not makers, of historical meaning. We also learn from the wonderful book by Urvashi Butalia titled *The Other Side of Silence* (1998) that the Partition was perhaps not even *always* treated as a horror. It might even have been a carnivalesque moment, an ironic inversion of the indignities that were routinely experienced by, say, the lower castes given their marginal existence in the village or town.

Now these are complexities to which historians have been increasingly attentive, to provide us with a fuller, richer, account of what was the inaugural moment of the Indian Independence, rather than the favoured binaries of the colonial past which have seen a revival in the present. What we are being asked to remember on 14 August is none of these nuances. We are being asked to remember one small side of the story to harbour it as a grievance and to be able to develop and inculcate the hatred of the other.

Let us turn to what the state increasingly would like our public discourse on Indian history, and particularly the history textbook, to be. I am referring to a document produced

by the Public Policy Research Centre
that compares history textbooks of
National Council of Educational
Research and Training (NCERT), the
Kerala and the Gujarat boards. The
report says that the NCERT textbooks,
produced after the NCF 2005, have
failed to give equal 'weightage' to all
people and regions of the country in
terms of representation. The report
does not refer to, or document, the lack
of inclusiveness here. Rather, it cites a
few examples from the Gujarat history
textbooks to demonstrate the 'right
kind of weightages'. Praising the
'correctness' of the Gujarat syllabus in
giving due 'weightage' to Hindu
historical heroes and epochs and

putting the Mughals in their 'right place', it also tries to suggest that there are aspects and elements of the past which need not be overemphasized. For instance, they suggest that the NCERT textbooks highlight and exaggerate caste difference. The point here is that the history book is obliged to produce a narrative of a continuous, glorious ancient past, broken only by the long period of what they describe as 'slavery', which includes, without distinction, and one must point out, ahistorically, both the periods of Mughal rule and of colonialism.

What is more interesting is the report's claim to scientificity, which is done by producing a number of statistical tables consisting of the number of times the words *caste, varna, jati, untouchable, gotra, shudra* etc. have been mentioned in the NCERT textbooks, and why this kind of emphasis is objectionable. They have also tabulated the number of times Jawaharlal Nehru has been mentioned as against mentions of Vallabhbhai Patel and Subhas Chandra Bose.

Ironically, protests against the content of the NCERT textbooks are routine, even though they cover maybe only ten per cent of the school network in India, because although the NCERT books are only recommended in CBSE schools, they have also been adapted and adopted by some state governments.

There were numerous objections to the NCERT textbooks, despite the fact that the new textbooks were intended to reflect the major transformations in ways of thinking about the history of the subcontinent. These transformations bridge the gap between the historian's understanding of history and academic scholarship of the past few decades, and what the students can be introduced to in a curriculum based on pedagogical needs.

The increasing pressure, from the side of the state on the one hand and the process of democratization of historical practice on the other, has urged many people to want to be represented in this national textbook.

But, given the fact that we are living in the age of information, can the history textbook actually teach historical method, rather than introduce students to specific forms of information? If that is the case, then what would such a textbook look like?

Let us take the example of the Class 9 Karnataka-board textbook. It introduces the 12th-century reformer Basaveshwara, one of the most important dissident figures of Karnataka history, who enabled the production of a very rich body of vachanas or prose poems in Kannada—the language of the people. Vachana Sahitya consists of the works of a large number of lower caste people, including women, who speak of their relationship to god. This was part of the Bhakti age, and Basaveshwara is somebody who is routinely taught in Karnataka-board textbooks. But here an attempt is being made to sacralise the historical figure by calling him 'Jagajyoti'. There is no attempt to introduce students to the ideas which were possible in the 12th century, through the inclusion and explanation of an actual vachana.

On the other hand, in the Kerala-board textbook, the chapter titled 'Revolutions That Influenced the World' begins with a poem by Kumaran Asan, who may be more familiar to school children. The poem is on the importance of 'freedom'. This chapter draws students into a discussion of the importance of freedom from a literary source and then goes on to discuss important revolutions such as the French Revolution and the American Revolution that have influenced the way we think about freedom.

Another interesting example is the way in which the Kerala-board textbook, while talking about the state's own past, is able to dissociate from a very narrow linguistic nationalism, which many states are prone to, by starting the chapter with a discussion on the Sangam poet Avvaiyar, from Ancient Tamilakam, and

the ways in which that history actually
relates to the history of Kerala. Here
we have an example of the textbook's
effort to break down linguistic
boundaries which may not have existed
in previous periods. It also introduces
the student to those cultural and
linguistic borrowings and exchanges
that might have taken place. The use of
Avvaiyar as a linguistic source places
Kerala's past in the region of
Tamilakam—a refreshing change from
the strait-jacketing of history engaged
in by competing linguistic nationalisms
and their respective state forms.

Very often our textbooks simply list
out the names of important temples.
This is not factually wrong, but it does

nothing except test a student's memory or capacity for recall. Instead, we could pose a series of questions about the importance of *why* rather than *what* and *when*. For example, instead of listing the multiple sites where temples influenced by Vijayanagar-period architecture are found (as in the Karnataka-board textbook), could we urge students to ask questions such as: What did these temples signify about the state patronage of religion? What do they signify about tolerance? What do they tell us about the wealth of donors? What are the kinds of artistic styles and skills and virtuosity that we can learn about from these temples? The Kerala-board textbook encourages such thinking, by urging and encouraging students to observe and make deductions from incomplete evidence provided in the textbook.

It is particularly interesting that the Kerala- and Karnataka-board textbooks think about ideas of time. For instance, the medieval period in the Kerala textbook is described as a period of exchange, not only on the economic and social planes, but also in cultural and political registers. That is completely different from the way the same period has been 'demonized' in recent times. By introducing such complex ideas of time, these textbooks show that Indian time reckoning is not linear. The following questions can introduce to students the cyclical idea of time: are there examples of cyclic or cosmological time even in our present? What are the examples of linear time? Can linear time be manipulated and if so, how? What are lengths of time covered in vamsavalis or family genealogies, and genealogies of eras, for example, the Shaka era? And finally, there is the important question about what memory does to time: time can be lengthened or shortened, depending on the historical example that is being discussed. All of these suggest a certain historical method. These questions can be raised about any kind of historical event or process.

I wish to give an example of the relationship between memory and history, and the kinds of sources—i.e. known or recorded historical sources—there are for people without a 'history'. For instance, Kumara Rama (1290–1320) is a folk hero and the son of Kampli Rama. In the Kampli region of Karnataka, he is remembered as a subject of six kaifiyats (historical records of villages or towns in the Deccan region) and innumerable folk tales, and worshipped as a deity in at least five forms. He is celebrated in jatras (folk theatre) and inhabits the living memory of people who inhabit the stretches from Kammatadurga to the Arabian Sea. Interestingly, the popular memory of this king, who is a relatively minor figure, exceeds that of the fabled Krishnadevaraya (of Vijayanagar fame). Hence, there are opportunities for bringing in local and regional histories in interesting ways which could make students think about the relationship between memory as a site of recalling a past (such as Kumara Rama's reign), as opposed to events and regimes for which there is an abundance of material artefacts and literary sources (such as Krishnadevaraya's time).

The discussion of state textbooks must also include the work done by Eklavya in Madhya Pradesh since the 1980s. The Class 8 history textbook talks about controversial figures such as Aurangzeb, but does not try to disguise or hide the very complex and contradictory figure that Aurangzeb was. We are introducing the student to his actions, but not in a simplistic way. Regarding Aurangzeb's jizya (tax levied on non-Muslim subjects of a Muslim ruler) and destruction of temples, students are encouraged to ask crucial questions, such as: If he really was a fanatic and destroyed temples and imposed the jizya, why did he not take these steps as soon as he became the emperor? Why did he feel that it was necessary to adopt such rigid policies against the Hindus only 10–12 years after he had been on the throne? What are the political and religious compulsions that drove him in this direction? Similar questions can also be raised about Tipu Sultan.

The future of India's past need not be bleak if we remain alert to the dangers of the supremacist state power that is swamping professional historical research and the teaching of history. For this, we must confront the contestations and ambiguities of our past, and we must nurture those 'steel nibs that are sprouting'. This is a beautiful phrase that I have taken from a remarkable collection of Dalit writings edited by K. Satyanarayana and Susie Tharu.

Perhaps this will now have to be done outside the institutional spaces with which we are more familiar, beyond the official proclamations and memorializations that are being promoted by the state in our diverse and rich nation. We must move in the direction of developing a historical temper—a new sense of the past that will allow our young to think historically and read a variety of conflicting sources in order to heal and reconcile. This is the need of the hour— to heal and reconcile—instead of staging afresh the battles of history, to help young people come to terms with India's conflicting pasts and to teach people that understanding and appreciation might be better ways to deal with the past than revenge and retribution. We certainly have immense resources to do this.

Notes

1   Walter Carruthers Sellar and Robert Julian Yeatman, *1066 and All That* (New York: Barnes & Noble Books, 1993[1930]), p. 85.

2   Sellar and Yeatman, *1066 and All That*, p. 92–93.

3   Sellar and Yeatman, *1066 and All That*, p. 114.

4   'Old dating system to continue in Tamil Nadu school textbooks', *The Hindu* (30 June 2018) (available online: https://bit.ly/41Llzbs; last accessed: 26 April 2023).

5   Pierre Nora, 'Between Memory and History: Les Lieux de Mémoire', *Representations* 26 (1989): 7–24.

6   'Full text of Pranab Mukherjee's RSS speech in Nagpur', *Mint* (7 June 2018) (available online: https://bit.ly/3V9D4iZ; last accessed: 26 April 2023).

7   Janaki Nair, 'Textbook Controversies and the Demand for a Past: Public Lives of Indian History', *History Workshop Journal* 82(1) (2016): 235–254; see also Maya Palit, 'The CBSE Just Removed an Entire History of Women's Caste Struggle', *The Wire* (24 December 2016) (available online: https://bit.ly/3HkJOFc; last accessed: 26 April 2023).

8   'Is Karnataka social-science textbook encouraging religious conversion? A fact-check', *Alt News* (5 June 2018) (available online: https://bit.ly/3L3WWzu; last accessed: 26 April 2023).

9   TED, 'Chimamanda Ngozi Adichie: The danger of a single story' (YouTube, 2009)

(available online: https://bit.ly/3LePnpO;
last accessed: 26 April 2023).

10 Janaki Nair, 'Speculations on the Rise of
the Public Anti-Intellectual' in Kumkum
Roy and Naina Dayal (ed.), *Questioning
Paradigms, Constructing Histories: A
Festschrift for Romila Thapar* (New
Delhi: Aleph Book Company, 2019).

11 E. H. Carr, *What Is History?* (London:
Macmillan, 1961), p. 20.

12 *The Report of the University Education
Commission (December 1948–August
1949)* (New Delhi: Ministry of Education
and Culture, Government of India,
1983[1950]), VOL. 1, CHAP. 2, §3, p. 18.
Available online: http://rb.gy/24ek0 (last
accessed: 3 October 2023).

13 Gyanendra Pandey, 'The Revolt of
August 1942 in Eastern UP and Bihar' in
Gyanendra Pandey (ed.), The *Indian*

Nation in 1942 (Calcutta: K. P. Bagchi, 1988), pp. 123–164; here, p. 136.

14 See 'Bhima Koregaon' on *The Caravan*: http://rb.gy/ttlkq (last accessed: 3 October 2023).

15 Editor's Note to *Dictionary of Martyrs of India's Freedom Struggle (1857–1947)*, VOL. 4 (New Delhi: Ministry of Culture, Government of India and the Indian Council of Historical Research, 2021).

16 Quoted in Muhammed Niyas Ashraf, 'When History is Held Hostage', *The Wire*, 3 September 2021.